Pseudo Love

By Mel Moore

PublishAmerica
Baltimore

ISBN: 1-4241-2465-4
PUBLISHED BY PUBLISHAMERICA, LLLP
www.publishamerica.com
Baltimore

Printed in the United States of America

Also by Mel Moore:

Silent Witness

Nature's Repose

Synopsis

It seems it is ok to write fiction, fantasy, surrealism and 'off the wall what ever you want to call it stuff', but don't write of abuse, not in UK anyway.

At a local college I was told that 'my TYPE of poetry' is referred to as 'Dark' or 'Gothic'. I don't like either title.

I write of real life and real things that happen every minute of every day to someone. Hopefully, this book will bring a realisation to many that we are out there in our thousands. You will swing through many moods, my work is not for the faint heart. Rather, it is a testament to all victims and survivors around the world. It is also to carry a message to those that would harm a child, by what ever means, Stop! Stop now.

Everything written here is taken from life, is as real as life itself. If anything here in my words relates to you or some-one you know, please find some-one to talk to. This book of poetry deals with every form of abuse, from child abuse, bullying, domestic violence, to death and the emotions and feelings left behind. I would like to think that every house had this book lying on the table or in the book shelf.

Young people would benefit if supervised, that is my opinion.

Bio

I was born in a small country town in the middle of the Cambridgeshire Fens, England, UK.

I was the baby of five children, my father left when I was three months old.

At twenty-one years of age I went into a very violent marriage with an alcoholic who was fourteen years my senior. Over the next seven years there was two more abusive relationships, one straight after the other.

I have been a foster carer for twenty-plus years and have always worked and lived with emotionally disturbed teenagers. My inspiration comes from them and my own experiences. When you hold a young person in your arms, that has just experienced night terrors because of abuse. When you have a child fall into your lap with exhaustion, because they just don't want to FEEL, anymore. When you look at a child with tears in its eyes saying to you, "Why" and you do not have the answer. Then you can feel a fraction of their helplessness. I hope here I can give you an insight into that world, the world of 'the abused child'.

Why do I write of such things? Because I was one of those that had no arms to hold me, no lap to fall into. I was a very nervous child, and displayed typical abused behaviour, but it was not seen, heard or listened to. So I developed speech problems at the age of six years, and found as I grew words was my love. Having had a speech impediment for many years and being unable to get across verbally what I wanted/ needed to say, I found words the perfect vehicle for the quagmire of emotions that had troubled me for so long.

Acknowledgment

I would like to acknowledge and thank all the children, young people and their families who live and have lived through hell because of the types of abuse and outcomes I write about.

[Yet I walk this earth, this plain of normality
Living this charade, façade, forever the impostor].

The poems in this booklet are a dedication to those around the world young or old alike.
If it is happening now or was fifty years ago, these poems are for you.
The strength you have in your inner soul is immense. God bless you and 'remember' you are not alone.

[Yet on the surface as the rose, gaily garb in summer pose.
Loving gentle, always giving, make-believe life she is living].

Pseudo

Creeping, lurking in the dark
Festering smouldering, stark.
Only to her it is obvious.
Only to her a hidden curse.
Like thorns barbed sting
Seeping poison to her bring.

Yet on the surface as the rose.
Gaily garb in summer pose.
Loving gentle, always giving
Make-believe life she's living
Meets a love to share her world
Then her story to him unfurled.

Brings distain upon his face.
Leaving her no sense of grace.
Inside this lovely lady dies
A little more alone she cries.
Only to her it is obvious.
Only to her a hidden curse.

Do We KNOW?

What of the child we say is "Fine"
Will our decision have reason or rhyme.
Shall we know for sure that child is all right.
He won't live the fears, some live every night
Do we know, no hand will hurt him, that he is safe inside.
Will his eyes tell in the morning, how many tears he cried.
When he's leaving for school will they notice
When he gets on the bus will they see
Will the bruises to all be apparent
Will his mates hear his unspoken plea.
When the teacher gets cross at his behaviour
Is detention the next step to take.
Will anyone look a little closer
Will we notice the pain and heartache
When he grows to a man what will happen
Will the circle be repeated again
Will some little child be happy
Will another child feel only pain

Little Boy

Brown ebony eyes seen nothing but tears.
Young life already so full of fears.
Trousers too big, broken shoes all worn.
Thin dirty body, you look so forlorn.

Bloodied face, mixed with dirt.
Endured pain, soul-destroying hurt.
Your house, your home such a disgrace
Scruffy little boy so sadly miss-placed.

He's drinking again you'll have to pay.
Tortured racked body, goes on every day.
The fear for you has become your friend.
Sharpened survival to you it will lend.

The cupboards are empty, no food to eat.
Inside your head you find a retreat.
Lost in a world relentless and cold.
Eight years passed, a life time old

Waves of Emotion

Waves of emotion cross over my mind
Over reason and barriers of time.
Surging in with relentless pain.
Washing over me never to wane.

Will the pain like the waves subside?
I fill an ocean with the tears I've cried.
Isolated shore that runs through my heart,
leaving me lonely, tears me apart.

The ebb and flow is liken to my soul
Upward, backward through eternity roll
Leaves no tranquillity or peace of mind.
Deep is the ocean with my heart entwined

I want to move on keep going back.
The future looks bleak, oft times black.
Will my soul be allowed to be free?
Or through eternity roll, as the open sea.

Enigmatic

Soulless times pass by me, through me
the craving from the womb for life,
A mistake! on the part of my soul.
It cheated me so, when my being, needed most.
Led me to believe that life was a blessing, a gift.
Not true, not at all, life is something that happens.
mostly, while you're busy making other plans.

My life and I, what to say about my life and I?
Hand in hand, not always a good arrangement.
But as 'Dr Jekyll and Mr Hyde' now you see me!
Mostly though 'now you don't', the ambiguous me.
No chemical-induced soullessness is needed in me.
I feel sometimes we have parted company and yet..
There is also a great compassion in me, for life.
Yet I fear it, as a concubine fears her master.
Soulless times pass by me, through me.
I live on, in hope, in anticipation

Ghosts and Shadows

Ghosts and shadows moving through my mind.
Like a country lane that will twist and wind.
Never to rest, never to die.
Never to end or even know why.

Why the ghosts still linger, not yet gone.
Shadows won't disappear when light is shone.
Why such an integral part of me.
Why do they refuse to set me free.

So much in my life, darkens my way.
Some hidden agenda to make me pay.
I try to see pleasure, mostly it's fine.
Then ghosts shadows, cross over that line.

Harbour of Love!

Stay awhile my child inside, stay awhile and sleep.
You are safe child inside, watch o'er you I'll keep
You suffered things no child should see.
Now you are safe the child in me.

What were they thinking, treating you so?
You were just a child, didn't they know?
They took your soul and tore it apart.
Were they so jealous of your innocent heart?

Drawn into their rancid world, you the chosen one.
Their web of deceitful lies, around you spun
They use your body for purposes obscene.
Left you feeling that you were unclean.
Stay awhile my child inside, stay awhile and sleep.
I will hold you in my heart if you need to weep.
The pain now only memories, I am fully grown.
Little girl inside of me, you'll never walk alone

So stay awhile my child inside you safely I will keep.
Know you are my child inside stay awhile and sleep.

He Blamed Her

Fists banging
Doors slamming
Mother screaming
Baby crying, crying

Furniture splinters
Fired up tempers
Mother shivers
Courage withers

A punch to tell
Mother fell
Baby yell
Temper swell

Feet flying
Body bleeding
Mother dying
Baby crying, crying

Police have come
Her life is done
He was the one
Who blamed her!

Just Another Child's Voice

She called "Mama" but she didn't hear.
She called "Papa" but he didn't hear,
clinging to the bars that made her prison.
Her strength denying her each hour that passed
unable to cry, just a little more than a murmur.

"Mama, Papa" no-one heard, no-one came
The stench of her young life surrounded her
in the dirty stain clothes and sparse bedding,
No food or warmth or a comforting word,
just a Child's voice that calls out in the dark.

Wide baby brown eyes brimming with tears,
face marked with the tears that have been cried.
One last call to her "Mama, Papa" no-one heard.
grubby little hands slide down bars that restrain her.
Gingerly sits on sore flesh, discomfort rife in her body

Once more she sits and waits for some-one to come,
for the warm milk, the love she has never known.
Her world a dark stinking room where little light comes
Her calls lost in the hum-drum as the world moves on,
just another child's voice lost in the dark, alone.

Living with Fear

The young woman was so angry
the day has been too long
All she had tried to achieve
has gone so badly wrong.

The letter shaking in her hand
says her marriage now is done.
We have given you custody
of three daughters and a son.

She's no idea what happens next
or how she's going to cope.
The last beating that he gave
left her very little hope.

She felt degraded so let down
the pain he caused was bad.
The brutal beatings she endured
now ended, made her glad

Now she found herself alone
four young mouths to feed.
Fear inside she knew with pride
she had to take the lead.

What other choice did she have left
there was no helping hand.
Just survive from day to day
and SURVIVAL sounded grand.

Speak to Me

I don't know, a twist of fate?
Such a nervous child, only eight.
Pains in my side, distressing stutter.
Try to speak, not a word to utter.

Gut retching, physical strain
Want to stay lonely, stand in the rain.
To be with my tormenters invisibly
Living my life silently

Body rocks, clenching of fists.
Do they see my eyes begin to mist
More speech therapy, doctors as well.
Cruel little world, my living hell.

No answer I give, the words won't come.
The answers there, they think me dumb.
Like a spinning top inside my head.
No relief, my mouth is dead.

Just a little girl, silent I'll be.
Anxiety and anger are rising in me.
Want to say no! "Stop the train".
That constantly crashes through my brain.

I hope one day I'll be heaven bound.
Live with the angels without a sound.
No voice I'll need for my heavenly start.
Just a golden trumpet and a little girl's heart.

Missing

Just keep driving in your car.
You're a danger, you know you are.
That child belongs somewhere else,
Don't act on a sudden, wrong impulse.

He has a family, people who care.
To take him from them, wouldn't be fair.
He is surrounded by love, people his age.
He's not an animal, to be put in a cage.

Don't slow down, just keep going by.
He's just a little boy, don't make him cry.
Your eyes the windows, to an impure soul.
Hunting for victims, quenches thirst to control.

Please don't stop, leave that child alone.
Your depraved world, he doesn't need to be shown.
Uncensored thoughts go round in your head.
You're about to do, what his parents dread.

Don't open that door, don't make him get in.
Can't you feel what you're doing, is a deadly sin.
Now the urge is excitement, he's in your car.
If you let him live, he'll carry the scar.

Anxious parents now stand by the door.
He's never been, this late home before.
Now it's dark and late, the streets deserted.
Father reaches for the phone, the police are alerted.

The little lad's gone, no-where to be found.
The police and parents, have looked all around.
All and the town-folk, will keep on searching.
For the one and the thousands,
Of kids that go gone missing.

Puppet

You crafted me, moulded me from birth
To make me forever your puppet, stooge
A shadow that haunts my every move
The world hanging over my head waiting.
To fall, crush, annihilate the pride in me.

Me Co Dependant, because of your lack.
Your fear of the world, kept me from it.
Gave me no self, no worth or honesty.
I lie somewhere between, here and there
A no-man's land not fit for habitation

You are there, forever now in my soul.
An abscess in the gut of my humanity
The blackness of bile rises in me
An attempt to cleanse, clear and purify.
To retch you from the essence in me, of me.

You gave life so you could possess.
Own and devour, the flesh of my being.
Now you are gone, puppet with no strings.
Stooge, no jokes to tell, no one to mimic
Left stranded, unable to move voluntarily.

I'm a Survivor

Things that happen to me.
I won't let them get me down.
I won't spend my life in misery.
Or wear a sadly frown.
I won't ever let them think.
That they have won the war.
I've nought to feel guilty about.
It's minds peace they're looking for.

I won't give redemption.
Or forgiveness they need.
I'll just carry on with life.
They can't hurt me. No; indeed.
They'll see I'm a survivor.
Not the child fore-lorn
I'll stop feeling hate.
Or regret, for being born.

My mind battles with reality
The body they controlled.
The outcome of such a tragedy.
Through the ages, was fore-told
They won't win a part of me.
My soul has set me free.
I'll steer my ship to safety.
Cause forever, I'll be me.

The Young Apprentice

Oh yes, I am what I am.
I have done the deeds.
Paid the penance for them,
Criss-crossed my life.
With sorrow and happiness.
Walked a narrow path.
Of guilt and restraint.

Yet it is because of you.
That I am, what I am.
Because of you, life made no sense.
No qualms about my persecution.
You have been my master.
Yet not on your own ship.
No master of your own, wicked destiny.

You should have left the creating to God.
Man has not the wisdom to create in his own image.
You have just created a mirror image.
An image of your own evil depths.
Now, compelled, propelled to do as you.
I groom my victims, to be my successors.
And so; the cycle moves on, you are dead.

I inherited your lies and deceits.
Now, as you I am an empty vessel.
No master of my own, wicked destiny.
No! Not on my ship!

Depths of Despair

Dear God! How can I free myself.
Free myself from this persecution.
This torment I meter upon myself.
I have become his collaborator.
A traitor to myself...to my very soul.

For I have seen things of violence.
Felt as a frightened child, full of pain, anguish.
Been beaten, maligned, taken to ungodly depths.
The depths of despair that only I know.
I try to please him, my persecutor.

I fear for my survival, my sanity,
Now as his collaborator, I see what he sees.
I am left feeling ugly, unlovable, stupid.
I feel burdened and let down,
My worth is that of nought.

In my mind I know, I am nothing.
For I have become my own judge and jury.
My own persecutor, my destroyer.
As he, my lover, holds me to the mirror.
Shows me what I have become, yes I see.

I have become nothing, not fit for man to see.
He is right, as he shows me the blade,
Puts it in my hand, I am numb, already dead.
Fifteen years he has tried to show me.
Show me my faults... my flaws... tried to teach me.

Yes, the lessons have been hard, and yes.....
I have felt as a frightened child,
I have been full of pain and anguish.
Beaten, maligned, taken to ungodly depths.
His words were, "For the love of you."

Now I must… free myself, from this persecution.
This torment…. I now meter…Upon myself.

Monument of Childhood

There it stood, cold and grey,
Can't really remember what it was for.
I think it was bad, because it upset people.
The grown-ups didn't like it, they cried.
It is nineteen forty-seven, I am six years old.
They have built this monument in the park.

It was a strange shape, should have
Been square, yet it has five sides.
Each had a large pinky colour panel.
With lots of names written on it.
I know they were names of people,
People who lived in our town.

They must have been scary people,
Grown-ups cried when they read it.
Said, "They won't be coming back."
Wonder why so many left, it's nice here.
A lot of people went to see it, they all cried.
I asked Mummy, "What is it," she said, "Hush!"

An old man was crying, he said to my mummy,
"There are three of my boys named there."
He wiped his eyes, "All gone, all gone."
I said, "Write a letter, maybe they'll come back."
"Hush," Mummy said, "Hush be quiet, now."
I don't understand, why is everyone so sad.

The old man wept, "They won't come back."
Then he bowed his head, sadly, low.
"I will be with them soon," he whispered.

Mummy took me home, will we be going too,
I wondered? I said, "pack my little bag?"
"Why?" she said, "they didn't leave, darling,
They all died"......................

"For what they believed in"...............
"The monument was built for them"........
I remembered asking, "How many?"
"Thousands," she said.
I didn't know how many that was,
But I knew it was a lot.
And they were all under there.......?
It is nineteen forty-seven, I am six years old.
They have built this monument in the park.

The Clock

There's a clock on a mantle-piece,
Been wound so many times.
It's scratched, old and battered,
Now doesn't know how to chime.
Look's like life's been quite unkind,
But the clock did all it was asked.
The beauty when new, still inside,
Though neglect, has got it masked.
Soon its usefulness will end,
It won't be needed anymore.
The card-board box is ready,
To take to the coal-shed-store.
In that shed its life will end,
In ugliness, not in pride.
One day, they'll ask,
"Where's the clock".
The answer will be, "It died"

Do You Remember?

Do you remember?
It was me, I was the one.
You made feel small.
You defaced my books
With your stupid scrawl.
No friends of my own.
I took the punishment,
all alone.

It was me, I was the one.
You hurt with your names,
Thought you were clever,
Playing your ugly games.
Didn't you see, pain in my eyes,
When you told the tutor,
Your stupid lies.

It was me, I was the one.
Who didn't achieve.
Cause you and your friends,
Gave me no reprieve.
Lived in fear each day at school,
Did you enjoy,
Being so cruel?

It was me, I was the one.
Who tried to die,
No-body knew, or guessed,
I hid away to cry.
Some-one hurt you,
So you made me pay.

I kept your secret,
And didn't say.

It was me, I was the one.
Who thought myself fat,
Ugly and a nerd.
Silently, I tried to let you know,
But you never ever heard.
You never knew, or saw the pain,
Each day I just died,

Brand-New Morning

It's a brand-new morning.
It's a brand-new day.
Feel like happiness.
Is coming my way.
Looked over my shoulder.
What did I see.
A brand-new day
Coming right back at me.
So many people
In a sorrowful plight.
Sadly won't make it.
Through one more night.
Addiction is rife.
Dependant baby born.
Struggling for life.
Looks so forlorn.
It's a brand-new morning.
It's a brand-new day.
Feel like happiness.
Is coming my way.
Looked over my shoulder.
What did I see.
A brand-new day
Coming right back at me.

Gifts

Here's a call to mothers.
And all fathers too.
Treat your children kindly.
For their a gift to you.
Love them, right from the heart,
Then a little more.
Don't treat their young demands.
As if they were a chore.

A human life you created.
Cherish it with pride.
Though your heart is weary.
Always be on their side.
When their life is really sad.
Others won't hear them plead.
Who could know them better.
It's you they really need.

Maybe they don't know it.
Tempers might even rise.
You'll see the pain and anguish.
Right there in your child's eyes.
You are the older person.
Seen things they haven't seen.
Walk your path, forged your rivers.
Been places they haven't been.

You've made mistakes and you know.
They're going to make them too.
Remember the helpless feelings.
These mistakes have left with you.

So here's a call to all mothers.
And all fathers too.
Treat your children kindly.
For their a gift to you.

Gothic-Dark or Fact?

The voice that comes quiet in the night.
Speaks of deeds unseen, obscene.
Muttered behind raised hands
Embarrassment lowers their heads.
The pen writes of unseen, obscene deeds.
Only to be clothe in a cloak of genres.
Gothic they say, Dark Poetry they call it.
Facts I call it, abusive I say, I write.
My senses are inflamed by this cloak.
This garbed protector of the abuser.
The voice that comes quiet in the night.
Speaks of deeds unseen, obscene.

Gothic they say, Dark Poetry they call it.
Facts I call it, abusive I say, I write.
Those that would walk, live in shadow.
Steal in the night for a child's love.
Walk the streets with their insane lust.
Brutalise, demoralise the fibre of society.
Give my words not a name for discretion.
Or camouflage for what lies beneath.
One that relays a message to survivors
One of brutal honesty, of truth, of fact
Gothic they say, Dark Poetry they call it.
Facts I call it, abusive I say, I write.

No Stone Marks Their Rest

~ ~ ~ ~ ~

The waves crash in with a mighty roar.
Spray-laden winds, tear at the shore.
I thought of ships all battered about.
Of watch-weary men, too hoarse to shout.
Slippery decks and a mighty sea.
Weather-worn sailors, pray for the lea.
Rigging all slashed lances the air.
Bodies tired, souls in despair.
Weather-worn wrinkles, salt-rubbed scars.
Oil-skins and jumpers for these old Tars.
Friends that were many, now lie beneath.
Their fate; as sailors before had bequeath.

When golden bells toll, resounding death rattle.
Mighty ships died, gone down, lost the battle.
Watery graves, no stone marks their rest.
The bravest of men, at their Captain's behest.
They called it the salty, the brine or the gravy.
But, proud were the men of the Merchant Navy.
Most of these men were quiet and kind.
With a simple heart and a humble mind.
Their fortunes at sea, they did fully embrace.
For they have gazed.... into their, God's face.

Teaching Them 'Right'

Rock that cradle with your love.
Tell stories from the heart.
Fit with your baby as hand in glove,
Your love to them impart.

For now you're at a thresh-hold,
The power belongs to you.
What they become in the future,
Depends now, on what you do.

Don't tell them of happiness missed,
Because they came along.
They'll grow-up with a heavy heart,
Think they've done you wrong.

Always be forth-right and honest,
Be gentle, kind and true.
If discipline has to be mention,
Make sure you carry it through.

Teaching them 'right' is their protection,
It may save their life one day.
I know you get tired and weary,
But make sure, it's not them that pay.

Restless Spirit

From out of the night came a deep, deep sigh
from someone with cares, too heavy to cry.
Soft on the wind like a lullaby.
And I wonder!

Whose heart's been burden with unshed tears.
To a sigh left wandering down the years
Long after this earthly life shed.
And I wonder.

Now time has swept the old house away.
There's no room now where the ghost can stay
And oh yes; I wonder.
I wonder......

Will that woman's soft sigh still break the night.
O'er the heaps of rubble and dust on that site.
Or will it homeless drift...always unseen.
How I wonder.

And if I go back there one weary night.
To keep a vigil on that dreary site.
Sense the aching troubles to this has left.
I wonder.

Would I hear my lady's sigh still shudder the air.
As it did for many a long past year.
In the dark and feeling more bereft?
How I wonder.

Has demolition freed her soul from the past.
And that sad, sad sigh, found peace at last.
I wonder.
Oh yes I wonder.

Blood Red

We had a good lunch, was full to the brim.
So we went for a ride, was too nice to stay in.
Down stony lanes lined with fresh spring grass
Corn fields are growing, winter's gone at last.

There's a field of tulips that we ride slowly by.
They look like a rainbow, playing truant from the sky.
Then way in front, glowed a field brilliant red.
As the breeze caught them, swayed each head.
They rippled and trembled like a sea of red blood.
Those tulips so bright, like soldiers they stood.

I sat and gazed while my memories wandered.
To another red field that people call 'Flanders'.
Too sad a thought for such a lovely day.
So I swallowed back tears, pushed the thoughts away.

We admired greatly, the colours going past.
Each new sensation seemed to better the last.
In my memory, I still see that field of brightness.
To my throat it brings a nostalgic tightness.
As I think of that field of red poppies that have blown.
On the graves of our lads, that no human hand has sown

Cotton Clouds

Little boy lying there
Young life all but done.
Tragedy surrounds your world,
The race for you is run.
Your soul chose a body,
That had an unfair start.
Fate played a trick on you,
Supplied a broken heart.

You watched the happy children,
Had your hopes and dreams,
But your cripple little body,
Only, writhes and screams.
As you slowly grow weaker,
Bad blood pulsates your veins.
Everyone's done all they can,
The end is all that remain.

Can hear your lungs are choking,
More drugs your only need.
Just a little longer,
Your frail body will be freed.
Close your eyes and sleep now,
That angel is your friend.
She will carry you on wings so soft,
And guide you through the end.

Step you lightly from your bed,
No pain is left in sight.
The angel came and called for you,
And took you to the light.

Your Mum and Dad are crying,
If only they could know.
You walk freely now on cotton clouds,
Your head wears a golden glow.

Message From a Mother;

I see nothing... here in my cocoon.
Hear sounds, noises, cramped difficult to move.
My limbs drag awkwardly through a fluid-like substance
I feel like... I'm floating

A hard jolt, a pressure startles me,
I feel threatened, upset, not sure.
Now unhappy with my world
Agitated, worried for my survival,
I feel weak and small, unable to fight.
I hear a muted voice, mumbling sounds,
Like listening through a wall, distant...

Today it told me it was my mother,
That it loved me, ask for forgiveness.
Another hard jolt, even harder this time!
It calms, I listened, something is wrong
The voice sounded sadder, quieter now,
It is crying, saying "sorry, sorry!
It will soon be over, soon be done".
"What will, is there some-thing wrong"?

The doctor is talking incessantly at her,
The young woman listens, partially so.
As he gives her the methadone, she cries
"Too late" he said, "Time for tears passed".
He is unfriendly, judgemental she feels.
Sad inside, as she talks to her unborn child.

She strokes her round body, in a circular motion.
"Soon be over", she whispers "soon be done".

Lowering her voice she continues.
"If you survive the withdrawal symptoms,
If they get your little organs to function right
If your weight isn't too light, your size too small."
"Then for me; Learn to laugh and play in the sun,
Don't do what your mother has done."
"Forget all the things you have inherited from me
Stay away from drugs, learn to be free."

My School

From seven to eleven I endured that school.
The people there were so very cruel.
The 'have's' said the 'have nots' were running wild
Physical punishment meted, on poverty's child.

The system these people were allowed to use.
Poor kids learnt early, how to handle abuse.
Forced in washrooms to wash before class.
'Clean Linda's' encouraged, watched through the glass.

Dirty Daisy's is what the 'have not's' were named.
The 'Clean Linda's' just children, played the game.
Linda's seated to the left , Daisy's to the right.
Didn't anyone see the children's plight?

What were they thinking, why was it not banned?
It could have been stopped with a wave of a hand.
Prejudice against poverty and mal-practice so rife.
Children could and was, being damaged for life.

Puppet

You crafted me, moulded me from birth
To make me forever your puppet, stooge
A shadow that haunts my every move
The world hanging over my head waiting.
To fall, crush, annihilate the pride in me

Me Co Dependant, because of your lack.
Your fear of the world, kept me from it.
Gave me no self, no worth or honesty.
I lie somewhere between, here and there
A no-man's land not fit for habitation

You are there, forever now in my soul.
An abscess in the gut of my humanity
The blackness of bile rises in me
An attempt to cleanse, clear and purify.
To retch you from the essence in me, of me.

You gave life so you could possess.
Own and devour, the flesh of my being.
Now you are gone, puppet with no strings.
Stooge, no jokes to tell, no one to mimic
Left stranded, unable to move voluntarily.

Take Care of Her

Her face bleeding soul aching.
How far had her pride fell?
Torment physical and mental.
For years she wouldn't tell.
His tongue as painful as his fists.
Killed her spirit held inside.
Fear sweeping over her life.
Like a never ending tide.

The happiness when they first met.
Was what she'd had prayed for.
She gave him all she had to give.
He just demanded more.
Anger was his master.
His drinking was her doom.
Given blame for sins not done.
He killed the flowers bloom.

Many times she meant to leave.
Now it really was too late.
His uncontrollable anger
Had turned her love to hate.
He took the only thing she loved
Tore it from this world
Lethal fumes blew in the car
Killed him and her little girl

Now she dreams of angels
A shimmering shining host
The little one right at the front.
Is the one she sees the most.
At night she stands by her bed.

Then lowers on her knees.
She asks those other angels.
To take care of her darling, please.

Sanctuary

Brutalised, victimised abandoned.
Abandoned by any hope of reprieve.
Any hope of being freed, understood.

I stay, linger, and wear this ring on my finger
I fear he and myself who put it on my hand.
Thoughts of our wedding day all now so far away,
No desert island dreams only what might have beens
Now, just an overwhelming sense of loss, fear
Loss of what might have been, fear of reprisal
For all that I do and all that I am, could have been

There were for me such hopes, such dreams.
The cream of my class, genius they said.
Then you came with your tainted love.
Your need to corrupt, control me some one

Now just a shell an emptiness of nothing
With what ferocity you de-humanised me
A pinprick of light fading, I, being consumed.
All possessed by the all-possessing
I retreat gladly, sadly to a place, my home
No one dares to come, inside I hide
In my own created loneliness.

Sorry Mummy

Poor mummy's going away again
the Doctor says she's ill.
She says I cause her too much pain
and have turned her life to hell.

She didn't want daddy to go away
and now she's stuck with me.
She said she wants her life back
it's not here she wants to be.

"Get out of my sight, move out the way"
she says through gritted teeth.
"you took those biscuits from the tin
you stinking little thief."

she screams and shouts, calls me names
I know that's not like her.
Then mummy has to slap me.
and that really makes her worse.

I get so clumsy, I don't take care
she shouts and screams, I just stare.
She tells me to stop, I just freeze
sorry mummy, I'm trying to please.

My writing is rubbish, paintings are bad.
Whatever I do just makes her mad.
"get out of my sight, you stupid child"
I run to my bedroom and try to hide.

I'm eight years old and not very bold
I'm afraid of storms and the dark.
I can't hardly talk, I stutter so bad
Mummy hates me, that makes me sad

The Dark Side of Night

When night comes calling and all is dark
neon light burst into life piecing the shadows.
Some are drawn like moths to a flame
to be scorch by their indecent proposals.
Thus they walk the dark side of night.
Quivering, shivering with their own delight
their thirst takes them on a wanton journey,
allied to shadows that night brings in her wake.

Innocent walks its dutiful path to find its rest
in safety away from the dark and shadows.
Unseen is the figure that hides, watches and waits.
The innocence's pathway merges with the shadows,
figure looming, stalking, attacks, innocent lost
Like a wounded sparrow fallen from the sky
thankful for life, no room for grace, she lost the race.
Broken, bleeding, no where to run, wanton journey done
Those allied to shadows that night brings, move on

The innocence's life has change, now more deranged
No more a dutiful path to rest, to survive is best
Mutated thoughts inside her head bears a dread
When night comes calling and all is dark

Unseen

She stands silently against the wall
Dirty pyjamas, matted tangle hair
Her little hands were brown as
the curls that fell on her shoulders.

Teddy bear's head protruding
Neck squeeze against her chest
Like her life depended on him.
Her only protector, her only solace.

She watches their every move
Liken to a rabbit ready to bolt
Her parents oblivious to her there
Continued their shared verbal barrage

Her thumb impounded in her mouth
The sucking movements change,
rapid to slow, tensing of the lips
drooping from a still, half-open mouth.

She slides along the wall, watching.
Her movements are slow, deliberate
Slips through the half-open door.
Gone, unseen, the barrage went on

Her little legs slowly ascended the stairs
one at a time, to a dirty, cluttered little room.
She sat Teddy on the urine-soaked bed,
next to Miss Cady and Primrose, her friends

Old yoghurt pots for cups, imagination for tea,
she quickly prepared a party for four,
Her mind in a state of limbo, she didn't hear,
wasn't aware, of the crisis ensuing beneath her

He, Him, They

There's a noose hanging around my throat.
Chocking the very life from me.
I can't think, I can't breathe.
My body shakes and sweats, help me please.

Physically I am fine and fit.
I run and move and play but
In my mind, my heart I am dying.
My soul taken away by he, him, they.

Day time in the sun I play.
In the night dreams are taken away.
My young body stiff and taut waiting.
Then in the devil walks and all dreams gone.

I keep my mind my soul on another plain.
Where none can reach not even he, him, they.
My body moves behaves reacts.
My mind and soul walk a separate path.

For my part, I feel as nothing, as his accomplice.
As his pawn with no mind of its own.
Each night I cry help me, please please…
Day time in the sun I play and play….

I Say Goodbye

In the church I stand nearby
Look at you, watch folks cry
No tears my eyes do depart
The tears I cry all in my heart

I follow your casket, one step two
Fine strong oak with golden hue
Inside this scene just you and I
Exterior existence my mind deny

Stepping slow this numbing walk
My woeful being at all does baulk
An angel to me from heaven sent
Your coil of mortality only lent

One red rose, I stand by your grave
Darkness descends, cascading wave
Soil heaped high, void open wide
As slowly down they let you glide

Strength now from my being gone
I hear the sound of the one voice song
Drains my sanity as they put you to rest.
'Morning has broken' was your request

flowered garlands at your head lie
I but left with the question why?
Lifeless silhouette, soul's courage wane
All that is left emptiness and pain

Wrenched from me all sense and will
Rainfall hide my lonely eyes spill
Body weakened I fall to the ground
Shattered heart breaks, without even a sound.

Little Cast Away

Just a little raggy doll perfect in making
Lovely face and fine blonde hair
Toes and fingers were all there

Such a precious little thing.
Lots of love did dolly bring.
Pleasure soon turned into stress.
Raggy doll, loved less and less.

Time went by an interest lost,
Much to little raggy dolls cost.
Not played or talked to anymore
Raggy doll cried, then cried no more.

United

She lay there quietly now, eyes closed
Wrinkled hands lying on the smooth sheets.
Waiting for him, friend, lover, husband.
Her bones old and decaying, mind feeble.

That is not what drains the life from her.
It is the monster inside that devours.
Started with a seed, it spreads and moves.
Like a train in a subway, relentless, unseen

She waits, for him, friend, lover, husband.
Fifty years, nothing could part or hurt them.
Life had been hard but they had each other.
Together they fought everything life gave.
Except this stranger, this marauder within

An old man sits in his chair, eyes closed
His bones old and decaying, mind feeble.
He sees her, woman, lover, wife of fifty years.
She smiles, he falls asleep for the last time.

Whisper

Whisper their names softly as you go.
Forget their faces not their glow.
Left by those people who once lived here.
Now eyes cold and dark just seem to stare.

Are you afraid of what's meant to be.
One day with those people will dwell you
and me.
In clay-laden ground for the endless sleep.
Whisper their names, remember and weep.

Tell Some-one

To kids bullied every where!

Boy skiving
Mother moaning
Boy groaning
Now hates school

Cold reminder
Detention teacher
Future bleaker
Resolve gets weaker

Trouble brewing
Group waiting
Gang threatening
Boy running, running

Weapons brought
Boy caught
They fought
Force to steal

Crime done
Police come
Boy run
Mother crying, crying

Golden rule
Don't be a fool
Go to school
Tell someone

Wrongly Accused

Lost everything, love banned.
Even my life, it seems unplanned
Just a soul looking for a life.
Found body torn with strife.

She allowed the sin, to go to far.
Now I am left to carry the scar.
Unwanted, unloved, mostly unneeded.
Myself, who I am, gone, now receded.

Now and then there's a glimpse of me.
The person I know I was meant to be.
Kind, gentle, loving and giving.
Then I get hurt, my soul stops living.

Parents love their children, for them toil.
Then bequeath, when leaving this coil.
Inherent in you hate and coldness.
Wrongly accused, I'm not worthless.

Where?

They're building again,
Land-fill again.
Will there be anything left
I wonder, I worry

Where will all the wild-life go
What about the plants
Where will they grow
I wonder, I worry

The country's filling up.
When will it stop.
The space may run out
I wonder, I worry

Farmers sell off land.
Should be taken in hand.
Where will food grow
I wonder, I worry

Could make fields smaller.
Animals with less space.
Would get fatter...quicker
I wonder, I worry.

Maybe kill them younger.
Twice as many bred, then...
More room for houses....people.
I wonder, I worry.

Keep them in smaller sheds.
Keep them there... till dead.
Will they be healthy? ...of course!
I wonder, I worry

They're building again,
Land-fill again.
Will there be anything left
I wonder, I worry

Who Goes There

Walking this path, I wonder, who walked here before.
No sign to be seen, not heard anymore.
Did they walk with a lover, or child holding hand?
Or like me stop; by this old tree and stand.
That bench over there, did they sit and cry?
Lonely their wait, till their love walked by.
Were battles fought, did some-one give up their life?
Did some dashing young man, propose to his wife?

In years to come, will it be the same for me?
Will some-one wonder, who stood under that tree?
Or, will it all end, will I be the last,
An echoing memory, down corridors passed?
Just a breath on the air…In somebody's dream.
Just to prove, not all things are what they seem.
But as long as one person, asks the question, why?
The past and her memories will never die

Tear the Heart

He snatched the child from my arms.
"You'll never see this little bastard again,"
He seethed through gritted teeth.
The fury on his face, his lips...froze me.
Like something possessed, the baby screamed.

Through my numbness and swollen face,
I could feel myself shake, hear myself say,
Over and over again, "I'm sorry, I'm so sorry,"
Empty arms reaching, pleading, imploring....
"Give him to me...please...give him to me."

The sounds and words came as a rasping breath,
My throat dry, mouth wet and throbbing.
To tear the heart from me, would be less painful.
Than to wrench my child from my arms,
The only good thing to come from this union.

This unholy match made in hell, forged from ashes.
He taunted me with the child, swinging to and fro.
I reached out, tried to secure him, keep him from harm.
As I move closer he jerks him away, laughing.
"I won't go, I won't leave, please," I begged, terrified.

One more movement away and then...and then;
He threw the child into my arms, we fell to the floor.
I cried tears of relief, the child screamed with fear.
"You'll pay for this," he snarled, glaring at me,
"I can't trust you now, you will never leave me."

I could feel myself shake, hear myself say,
Over and over again, "I'm sorry, I'm so sorry,"
The fury on his face, his lips…froze me.
Like something possessed, the baby screamed.

To Be or Not To…

There's a kinda hush all over the world
A kind of silence as the story unfurls.
The dying has stopped, warring is done.
Bloodshed claimed the last mother's son
The quietness seeps all over the earth
Nothing is left no seed to give birth
Winds now blow down empty streets
No men no planes no mighty fleets

Shutters bang helpless on unpainted frame
Each street like the last, looks just the same
Rich man poor man now equalled score
No one to look up to, no one to abhor
Lonely playgrounds stark and grey
Gone are children that once did play
The world surrenders, life has gone
The day has come the sun hasn't shone

Special Child

~I would like to dedicate this poem to a special boy, that is very special to me. His music is his love and one day he will show the world, what a special child he is. Well done, Jamie, we love you!~

His mind's not clear his feelings mixed
he wonders if he'll ever be fixed
Old beyond his years, just a lad,
his clumsy ways make him sad

He's full of love and silly words
fantastic stories quite absurd.
He tries so hard just to please,
but total support meets his needs

He seems content as he fumbles along,
the more he tries, more he gets wrong.
Totally lost in his world of confusion,
Normality, just another intrusion.

I walk past his room, hear him cry,
I try to consol him, he asks 'why'?
Fluctuates between angry and very mild,
doesn't understand, he's an Autistic Child

He asks all the time, why he's this way
soothing words is all I can say.
I tell him that he's as special as can be,
And one day others, will see what I see.

What Is Love?

What is love? The beast that raises its head
and allows one human to exploit another?
The urge inside to become half of a whole
Regardless of pain or treachery?
The feelings for one's self that makes us
Abandon sense, reason, wife, husband or child.

When ladylove wraps her fingers around your soul.
Does it depend on whether they are fired with passion
Or cold as slithers of ice piecing
with doubt and suspicion?
Is love such a lottery or game of chance?
Or is this only the one side of a coin?

Is love in the eyes that meet a crossed the table,
the caressing of a cheek or the holding of hands?
The tears at the station, the smiles at the church,
holding the unwashed body of your just-born child?
Now, I feel the warmth rising in me
As if to give thought to love is to give it birth.

Much to ponder about love; it is a strange event.
Charging me through with emotion.
Raising me up to such heights of elation
Then dashing down to depths of despair.
Oh love, only you, can force this blood through my veins
as sap to a tree, bringing life each spring, each love.

Why Do I,

I've looked after children for many years.
There's been lots of laughter and lots of tears.
It's never been easy and that is a fact.
Lots of diplomacy, never-ending tact

My status is ambiguous, loop-holes galore.
Meetings, legislations can be a chore.
You just get it right, it all changes again.
Departmental Reorganisation? Oh! what a pain.

Dentists and doctors medicals and schools.
Specialists and social workers all with their rules.
Strangers and families all come to your house
Contact meetings, they all have their grouse.

Any carer out there will know what I mean
What's printed here is barely half of the scene.
Impossible, outrages the kids never gracious.
In fact quite rude and downright audacious.

Then there are time's when you get it just right.
You look in the eyes, see the panic and fright.
They are angry confused, in pain, cuss and shout.
But we know that's not what it's really about.

They are lost in a world between here and there.
Wondering why strangers could possibly care.
I wonder too, ponder for a while.
Them my fax machine sends me another kid's file.

Nursery Rhymes?

Star dust from angels' wings
Mocking bird begins to sing.
Princes and princesses fall in love
Live in castles on hills above

Witches and wizards casting spells
Imagination in children wells
Round-about and a ghostly ride
Monsters in your cupboards hide

BFG's reached into child's room,
Hansel and Gretal, were the witch's doom.
Dinosaurs are back! Taking over the planet?
Dorothy's enemy was stone-faced granite.

Ogres giants and ugly trogs
Bewitched princes turned to frogs.
Super heros keep demons at bay
What to children, are we trying to say

Children whisked off, away from their home,
Turn into donkeys if they dare to roam
We tell these tales, then look surprised
When they go to bed and can't close their eyes

When?

When does one stop being a child?
When does one stop wanting to hide?
When does your fear turn to faith?
When is the damage, at last restored?

Is time all it really takes, then how long?
The spring of one's life, when all is new?
My spring, was laden heavy with dew.
The summer, when rainbows are so bright?
Most summers for me were dark like night.
Autumn now at open gate, for me too late?
Is time all it really takes, then how long?

True the sun has now absorbed the dew.
Colours in rainbows, seems now renewed.
Autumn is yet to state her case, I wait.
Will she remove the con from confusion?
Will I at last, blend, Merge, unite?
Be one, with the one I was to be?
No more the child, or wanting to hide.
Fear becomes faith, damage restored.
Ahh, the stuff dreams made of....

Only Children

Somewhere in my memory
the fields of Norfolk were as home.
Sitting in cultivated flowers
Picked for bridal bouquets
Lying, in rows of strawberries
crying, amongst gooseberry bushes
sleep a Child's sleep, under apple trees.

No mummy's kisses, daddy's smiles
not for me, not for us, time was money,
No fun-fairs or donkey rides.
Just mother somewhere over there
as she picked, planted and sowed.
We came and went as did the seasons
as did the reasons for being there.

My sisters two, were older than I,
Father long since departed, gone.
They worked as women, no mercy.
Only children mis-placed, ill used
Whilst I cried with heat or cold.
No swimming lakes or picnics,
Summer fun, no fun in the fields.

I a baby then, at the disposal of
Those who would control me, my life
I waited to be fed, cared for, loved
Sitting day after day in the fields.

As I became older, I remember
I played my part, the larger scheme
Only a child mis-placed, ill used

Schools played a part in the master plan.
holidays to accommodate the seasons.
Children to work six days a week
bolster the parents coffers, relentless.
Our reward was to be clothed and fed.
Little else, no love, no respect, yet
respect was always demanded of us.

Though few of them, earned respect.
The foulness of their mouths and minds
Not for young ears, they paid no mind.
It was hard times with harder people.
Children left to mercy, exposed to these
Moral-less men and women, the men…
Groom us with treats and candy.

The women blamed us, complaints loud.
Their abuse constant, tolerance negligible
Yes we were to blame for some, yes.
We were children in a harsh world
A grown-up environment, no place,
no place for young hearts and mind.
Only children mis-placed, ill used

Nobody's Child

Know, I'm just a little child
Afloat in a world of big people.
I know I'm not pretty or smart.
I never will win any hearts.

Nobody keeps me just because.
I'm bad sometimes mummy said.
I scare easily, scream at spiders,
Spill my food and wet the bed.

I like it sometimes being bad.
People talk to me, find my company.
Sometimes they shout, I don't mind.
I have their attention and they're time.

If I'm with you just for a while.
I'll draw you pictures make you smile.
Have a picnic in the park for tea.
We could pretend, you love me.

Tribute to Porgie

I looked at you in those last days, just a shadow.
A shadow of what you used to be, so strong and proud
You chose me from all of the rest, I belonged to you.
No doubt, what was behind your eyes when you look at me.
Those soft brown eyes watching across the room, held my gaze
You belong to me and yet I only ever see you as a friend

By the sea-side you followed me into water way out of your depth.
Had to keep you at shore for your own safety while I swam.
Then you whimpered and whined till I was back safely with you.
Oh my darling boy, what happened, where did the years go.
When you were born at my hands, no vet in sight then, only me
You and your mum, she in a lot of pain and getting worried.
So I did what needed to be done, I thought you so beautiful.
You got older, I realised how beautiful your soul was.

They said he's just a canine, just a dog, what did they know.
I took you to that surgery you walked beside me, trusted me
I said good bye to the best friend I ever had in this world.
Your head laid in my hand and you fell asleep, for the last time
No-one in my life ever showed me such loyalty, my darling friend.
I will miss you so very much, I can't imagine this house without you

Obscurity

Slipping away, just slipping away
Inside I hide, safe from harm.
I sway and move like a tree
Caught in the cross wind, I am free
You can't hurt me anymore, not you
With your condemnation or brutality
your brashness or your immorality.

You have polarised my very being
two, yet one and the same she and I.
She is all that is brave in me, accursed
I am not strong, I will slumber for now,
only now lest I should die by her hand,
the undoing of me, my fantasy.
My mind, soul, departs, from she.

Gone now, from the warped part of me,
facade she lives, presents, so I survive.
I ensconced in my non-reality, my figment,
leave her to be the semblance, order of me.
My parallel illusion now held firmly at bay.
uniformed bars surround my world, my mind.
I, not she, sink into obscurity, mindless, safe

Tormented

Inside my heart is still dying
I spend my life just trying.
To forget the things you did.
When I was just a little kid.

Didn't you know I was scared
That it was you that I feared?
Your persecution so very real.
How terribly small you made me feel.

Put me down, showed me rage.
I was such a young tender age.
You loved my sister and my brother.
Did you forget, you were also my mother?

Bullied so much when at school
did you stop them, being so cruel?
Each day I came home crying in pain.
The bullying started all over again.

Shattered nerves, no one knew why.
All the time I would sit and cry.
Hurt by you when reviled
I didn't understand, I was just a child.

All I did you thought was wrong.
I wished like you to be strong
I loved you so, couldn't you see?
Your lack of love just tortured me.

You lay there dying in your bed.
regretting things you once said.
I sat and listened to your plea.
Ambiguous feelings, but I set us free.

Two Little Girls

'For the Two Little Girls in the National Papers today'

Two little girls clung together, hearts without hope.
Made a pact with each other, with life could not cope.
One was plump with freckles, the other glasses and tall
Each day in the playground, they felt so very small

It started about a year ago, a story they could not tell
A gang of girls sought victims, to turn their lives to hell
The plump girl their target they cared not about age.
Then a yearlong battle that quickly turned to rage.

They tore her coat, pushed her down, chanting "run run run".
A tall girl called a teacher, they said "it's only fun".
Teacher gave detentions, they looked at her with hate
Started the yearlong obsession, ended with a twist of fate

Two little girls cling together, saved pills swallowed inside.
A pact made with each other to end the tears they'd cried.
Adults said "Just ignore it," the gang said they'd both liedTwo little
girls together, sat alone in a shed and died.

Why, Daddy?

Why did you hurt me, daddy, came the plaintive plea?
Was it cause I was a bad you've done this, to me?
It's not just my body, my heart feels very sad.
You took my mummy away, and everything I had.

My sister left awhile ago, she went with a lady too.
Mummy got cross, "Take her! There's nothing I can do,
my husband is a good man, he couldn't do what you say,
She just hates her daddy, and I'm going to make her pay".

I had to go to hospital, and stay there for several days.
Lots of stuff was going on, it's like being in a haze.
A policeman and a woman, walked in with a smile.
"We'll take you to a new place, to stay there for a while".

Don't know what they're saying, it all seems like a dream.
They say you can't go home, I want to sit and scream.
They've asked me lots of questions I promise I won't tell
Have you been naughty, daddy, is that why you're in a cell?

I'm sitting in this strange place, some one else's house.
They say you're a wicked man, nothing but a louse.
What's happening to me, daddy, can my mummy come?
I hear the lady talking, saying bad things on the phone.

She takes me to a little room she says it's where you'll sleep
"This is now your new home" I just want to weep.
What happened to my old home, did someone take it away?
I think this is a nice one, but I really don't want to stay.

Whatever they say, daddy; I love you with all my heart.
I think about you, daddy, even more, now we're apart.
I'm your special little girl, your little angel too,
I'll be here a long time, there's nothing I can do.

I don't understand

I am angry, with myself, maybe
If not then who, my mother.
Who tore me, my life to shreds?
Left nothing of me worth having.

My father, womaniser that he was.
Who left me to her mercy, no mercy?
Walked away to a new life, (child).
Leaving the old, (me) behind.

Can you replace a child, a daughter?
How do you replace one for another?
Unwanted human garbage, waste?
Send it back to where?

Was the new she, prettier than I.
Maybe she was a better baby.
Didn't cry, or make a fuss, did I,
Did they see the mark upon me?

Is that why no matter how I try?
I find no worth in myself, no pride?
Nothing to be proud of, stand tall by
Then why do I try, why do I continue?

I have faith in myself with no foundation
A belief in myself with no substance.
I fool myself with promises of tomorrow.
Tomorrow is forever away.

Where Are You?

All my life I looked for you, your essence.
Loves came my way, soured then left
Then there you were so sure of yourself
Yet I didn't know, couldn't have guessed

I came to know as you did without doubt,
Grew to love you, feel you, sense you.
I loved you, laid with you, gave you my life
as you did yours to me, we were as one for so long.

Then a veil lighted upon you, moved you from my side.
Yet still I sense you, reach for you, where are you?
You are the sun on my face, the rain on my skin.
You are forever my love, my music, my life

Why?

Why does my pen continually write?
When I open my mouth
All words are gone

I feel my breath panting
My chest moving up and down
In a quickening fashion, rapid.
My stomach turns brain churns.

I try to speak, words escape me.
It is not my sin my shame
Yet an invisible hand
Grips me, silences me

A child needs help
I do what I must do
As a fellow passenger
Then I see, yes I see
What I do next for this child
Is my voice, my words?
I have spoken…

I Feel

I feel…. Feel, what! Do I feel.
Exhausted, soulless, a lump in my chest
Like a growth of huge proportions,
I can't breathe, intakes of breath are so painful
My heart just brims over at the thought of you
The thoughts of when we were together,
Oh my darling; I am so very sorry for what I did.
I wish you back with all my heart, I want you here.
I miss you moving around me, with me.

Angel

~This poem I would like to dedicate to my daughter
Katie Moore. I would like to tell her how proud I am,
when I look at her and see the beautiful young
woman she has become. Thank you, my darling, for
being my daughter.~

I look at her just lying there.
I can't tell anyone what I fear.
I want to walk, away.
I want so desperately to stay.

Can I do this again, again.
Don't touch me don't look at me.
Leave me cocooned inside while.
I pray for her, breathe for her.

She is untouchable, so unreachable.
Never has anything been so loveable.
Four centimetres of glass,
one mile for my heart.
I can't breathe fear binds me.

I watch her little chest pulsate.
First slow, then fast, then slow.
Eyes flicker behind closed lids.
She wants to survive I sense it.

She has fought longer than the rest.
Three days old her battle strengthens her.
She has a chance they say.
I want to retch, to vomit, to cry.

Many little souls came and went.
She lingers longer, grows stronger.
My body is damaged now barren.
She is my sole survivor.

Angel on My Pillow; Trilogy

(1)

There's an angel on my pillow, right beside my head.
There's an angel on my pillow, that's what mummy said.
She said if your heart were hurting, they'd see what they could do.
Angels on your pillow can make your wishes come true.
So I going to ask that angel, the biggest wish there could be.
I going to ask that angel to bring my mummy back to me.

(2)

There's an angel on my pillow, there's an angel on my bed
Are angels really angels, or people who are dead.
Are they like a rainbow, brightening up the sky.
Are they in a ladybird or a beautiful butterfly?
Are they in some people, a thought crossed my mind.
I have met some people that are beautiful, angelic and kind

(3)

There's an angel on my pillow, there's an angel at my side.
Helps to think she's standing there, when life makes me tired.
When I feel I've suffered, can't really take any more.
I hope my little angel will open up the door.
The door will lead to a garden, much beauty there to see.
I know my little angel has reserve a place for me

Fallen Angel

Took your first breath, cried a little
Straight from someplace beautiful
So perfect in shape and make
Little angel dropped out of the sky.
Where you land is of utmost importance.

Will you ride rainbows from your mother's heart
Swing on stars in her eyes given by you.
Dream of candy floss and cotton wool clouds
Will you be the princess in her story or…

Is your destiny to be, just another mouth to feed?
Hungry little girl in a great big hungry world.
Will your heart ache with loneliness.
While fearing those that should love you best

Down the passage of time we will hear your cries
While you slide away inside to hide
No princess in glory, just another sad story
One that will be told, whilst angels weep

Some-one Pays!

Newspapers today came through the door,
all I read was crime, burglaries galore.
Fighting, cheating doing as they please
their names in the papers, do it with ease.

A child took her life, a bully had fun,
Now her young life, over and done.
Bully went on a trip to broaden his mind,
Child's family forgotten left grieving behind.

Some people in society think it's alright,
to drink on Saturday and start up a fight.
Hear them joke, think it's funny
their future is bleak, not very sunny.

They'll see too late, there's a price to pay.
If they keep going the same old way.
Old lady was robbed, I read of her plight
Now she's afraid to go out at night.

Young girl was raped, lost her fight for life.
little boy with no mother, a man no wife
A collection was made for a child that is ill.
money was stolen to buy dope and pills.

What's happening, in our world these days,
Don't they know, that some-one pays
Newspapers came through the door today,
all I read was crime, all I felt was, dismay.

Printed in the United States
55533LVS00006B/289